I Am a Citizen of the United States

Nancy Anderson

Rosen REAL READERS

I0809766

Rosen Classroom™
New York

My name is Chris.

I am a citizen of the United States.

I was born in Arizona.

Arizona is a state.

It is in the southwest of the

United States.

My mom and dad are
United States citizens, too.
They were born in California.
California is on the west coast of
the United States.

United States citizens have rights. These rights are written in the Constitution.

This is my friend Rubén.
Rubén was born in Mexico.
Mexico is south of
the United States.

Rubén and his family
are our neighbors.
Last year, they moved
from Mexico to the United States.

Rubén and his family moved to Arizona.

They wanted to become citizens of the United States.

Rubén and his family learned how to speak English.

They took a test about the United States.

Rubén and his family
passed the test!
They are now citizens
of the United States.

Rubén is in my class.
We say the Pledge of Allegiance
at school.
We are proud to be citizens
of the United States.

Words to Know

citizen

Constitution

dad

family

mom

test